QUIETLY WILD

QUIETLY WILD

POEMS, PHOTOGRAPHS, AND RITUALS TO MARK THE SEASONS

ALIX KLINGENBERG

MANDALA

SAN RAFAEL LOS ANGELES LONDON

*This book is dedicated
to planet Earth,
and most especially,
the trees.*

CONTENTS

INTRODUCTION	8
A PERSONAL WHEEL OF THE YEAR	10
September	13
Ritual of Letting Go and Calling In (Mabon/Autumn Equinox)	22
October	29
Ritual of the Thinning Veil (Samhain/Halloween)	42
November	45
December	59
Ritual of the Longest Night (Yule/Winter Solstice)	69
January	75
Ritual for Integration (New Year's Day)	76
February	89

Ritual of Poetry and Fire (Imbolc/Deep Winter)	91
March	105
Ritual of New Beginnings (Ostara/Spring Equinox)	114
April	121
May	135
Ritual of Flowers (Beltane/May Day)	136
June	149
Ritual of the Longest Day (Litha/Summer Solstice)	159
July	165
August	177
Ritual of Bounty (Lammas/Harvest Season)	178
ABOUT THE AUTHOR	191

INTRODUCTION

We each have our own seasons, both geologically and meteorologically speaking, as well as on a more personal, metaphorical level. This book is an exploration of both the seasons of the year, as we traditionally think of them, and also the seasons of our lives.

Getting into alignment with our natural environment is a key component for well-being and joy. Studies have shown that allowing yourself to change with your own internal rhythms helps prevent burnout and mental and physical illness, and increases self-love, peace, and meaning. I believe it is also a way for us to bring more attention to our planet, to the many incredible plants and animals we live alongside, and to the human animal's impact on our own home.

The rituals in this collection follow the path of Earth as it travels around the sun, marking the equinoxes, the solstices, and the midpoints between. They coincide with the Pagan holidays of the year (Mabon, Samhain, Yule, Imbolc, Ostara, Beltane, Litha, and Lammas). However, I am approaching the rituals with a religious naturalist lens. Where humanism puts humans at the center of ethical concern and reason as the highest value, religious naturalism puts nature at the center, with humans as only a part of the whole. Where Wiccan and Pagan traditions use gods and goddesses as metaphorical embodiments of natural aspects, religious naturalism believes that nature is enough, in and of itself, to inspire worship, awe, and humility.

My hope is that this collection will help you pay attention to and reconnect with the wild animal within yourself. I believe that we are integral parts of nature. That humans are just as much creatures as wolves or foxes or whales. We have ingrained rhythms and drives and wildly intuitive senses. We are uniquely capable of language, of using tools, of creating community, and of learning from one another. We make art, we make meaning, and we pass down our learning to the next generations. Quietly Wild invites you to investigate what it means to be spiritually grounded in the natural environment.

A note about my own physical seasons: I live in the Northern Hemisphere, and these poems draw mostly from my current experience living outside Boston, Massachusetts, but they also include some references to Illinois, Ohio, and California. I've also included the corresponding months for those who live in the Southern Hemisphere. I hope you will be able to enjoy and find meaning in them regardless of where you live.

I am beginning this book in September, because that is when the year feels like it begins a new cycle for me. You can begin the book wherever you'd like—your birth month, January 1, or wherever you are in year when you decide to open this collection!

Sincerely,

Alix Klingenberg

A PERSONAL WHEEL
OF THE YEAR

As we begin, I invite you to go through your year and think about what each month holds for you personally, professionally, and in your family system.

Write down each month and think about birthdays, vacations, summer camp, work trips, etc.

Then consider:

- How does your energy flow in each season?
- When are your best months for creative work, and when are you swamped with other things?
- What are your major holidays and traditions?
- When do you need lots of rest?

I invite you to use this book to help you create your own wheel of the year and begin to honor your own seasons!

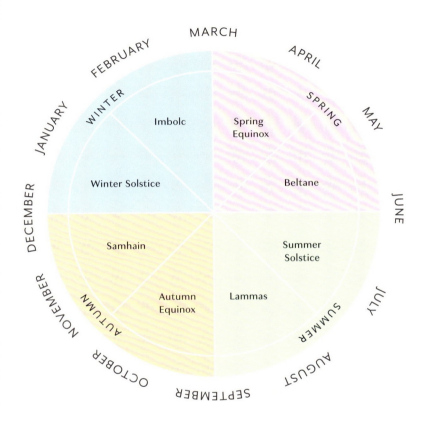

*I follow the seasons,
and my heart.*

A Personal Wheel of the Year

SEPTEMBER

Summer days and autumn nights—
in September we move from greens to oranges,
poised on the edge of night and day,
a time to find our equilibrium.

Quietly Wild

Let's reject the productivity culture
that leaves our souls exhausted.

It's time to rewild and reconnect
with our internal rhythms,

to honor our animal natures
so that we might see ourselves with clarity,

beings of the Earth made from the stars.

September Is an Invitation

Make some tea with lavender and honey.

Take a bath with Epsom salt and

any music that soothes you.

Stand barefoot in the rain.

Take pictures of the trees.

Soak in their late summer joy,

their deep green smiles.

Let your little earth soul be so full.

Let it all be too much

for you to hold.

Let it all be overwhelmingly good.

A Poem for the First Day of School

You get a haircut and some new
long-sleeved shirts. We pick up
pencils, a sharpener, markers,
and adult scissors.

We write your name in black ink
on blue plastic, on the tags
of your sweaters, on masking tape.

Six folders of various colors
and your red backpack filled
to the gills with fresh starts
and sharpened graphite.

May your teacher smile with their eyes,
may your best friend be in your class,
and may you have the desk next to the window,
or near the front, or by the kids you like.

May the day be full of laughter
and welcome and fun.
May you come home smiling
and melt on the couch,

ready for another year of becoming
your beautiful, unique, creative,
hilarious self.

Autumn's Keeper

The path is a river of pine cones,
red and ancient as the squirrel's tail,
hushed as a night warden making her rounds.

The red fox is waiting for you to remember
this is not a dream, not anymore.
There is a circle of pines and you
at the center, shining
in your russet cloak, brass buckles
at the neck.

You came here a mother
and left a hunter
emblazoned with a crimson purpose,
to light the chalice of change.

Cucumber Season

The wind is a whistling kettle
at the window,
a kind of alarm to signal
the end of summer days.

The birds are quieter and more busy,
doing their bird business between the neighbors' rooftops.
I am not sure what they do for work,
the birds or the neighbors,
but I wonder if they watch me in the morning,

barefoot and wearing only a T-shirt,
wandering out to check on my garden.
The cucumbers are round this year,
perfectly round spheres,
like they decided to come out as women
after years of playing men in grocery stores.

I wash one off, removing the sharp spines
that keep the deer from eating them all,
and cut them into phases of the moon,

sprinkle them with sea salt,
and see if they taste as feminine
as they look.

They taste sweet and warm,
like sun-ripened cucumbers do,
like women do when they have enough time—
when they can make themselves into
any shape that pleases them.

September, September

She slips out the window
one foot then the other
into the shining swell of summer.

"September, September" she sings
with a sigh, I remember the paths lined
with soft, fallen pines.

The swelter of summer gives way
with a shudder,
a shimmy,
a rustle of wind in the cedars.

She breathes in the breezes,
the peat moss, the lichens,
"September, September" she softens
and slows, the trees stop to listen,
the river it flows.

They whisper of secrets and endings
and rest, and she lays down her burdens,
and striving, and stress.

SEPTEMBER 19–22 (MARCH 20–23)

MABON/AUTUMN EQUINOX
Ritual of Letting Go and Calling In

Materials you will need: a piece of paper, a pen, a way to burn paper safely (a candle and a little bowl of water to put it out, a fire pit outside, a match lit outside, etc.)

On your paper, make two columns: one that says, "Let Go," and one that says, "Call In."

Take 5–10 minutes to write down some things you'd like to release as you move into this new season, and some things you'd like to welcome or invite in.

Example:

LET GO	CALL IN
my fear of failure	more ease and joy
my need to prove myself to my parents	more physical movement
my limiting beliefs around money	balanced friendships
clutter	unbound creativity
clothes that don't fit anymore	health
my fear of being misunderstood	presence with my son
	welcoming community

Cut the lists into two separate pieces of paper, and then light a candle. Take a few deep breaths and read aloud what you are letting go. Really feel what it would be like to fully release these things as you say them. Then, burn the Let Go paper and let all of those things release into the ether.

Take another few breaths and then do the same thing with the Call In paper, imagining each item on the list as fully as you can. You can save this paper as a reminder for yourself, or, if you feel like speaking them aloud is enough, you can burn this one, too.

Autumn's Altar

We begin with a ritual,
on the threshold
of light and dark,
day and night.
We rest our heads on the altar
of autumn
and come back into balance with
our whole selves.

It All Just Shifted

Did you feel it?
Do you feel the new air,
the subtle but insistent relief,
like a song you know coming
on a playlist of unfamiliar tunes,
like the smile of your best friend
after months apart,
like the gentle nudge of your cat's
head under your palm.
It's here.
It's here.
You're here.
You're alive.
And suddenly, silently,
you're okay.

September Is for Self-Proclaimed School Nerds (No Matter Their Age)

new shoes

new pencils

new notebooks

new outlook

new possibilities

and a return to the comfort of routine

ivy-covered bricks

and freshly brewed coffee

the sound of pages turning

in the library

and the gentle chatter of new friends

we wait all year for this

Stay Here with Me, September

September is the turning point,
the tilt of the Earth on her tiptoes,
the slow drift toward darkness and rest
and night, but not quite

yet.

You hold the world in place with a finger
to your lips, the tip
of a chin,
the slight gap
between your teeth,
the moment before the inevitable kiss—
magnetic, full, and heavy with almosts.

Stay here with me, September.
Stay poised on the edge of satisfaction,
the brilliant agony of almost falling,
the pain of beauty too precarious
to last.

OCTOBER

It's okay to be still for a while,
to sit in the October sun
and just bask in a dream
made manifest.

Earthkin

She was Earthkin, a forest walker—

tuned in to the fox den and the sparrow nest.

She talked to the maple tree on the corner

by the bookstore, whispered secrets into the stony bark.

And it spoke to her in hushed leaves

of the coming autumn,

of letting go,

of small deaths.

She felt herself shedding layers,

preparing for her own kind of fall.

Autumn Ivy

I swear to you,
everything can seem terrible
and lonely and horribly mundane,
and then you see the autumn ivy
curving in great rainbows
around the cemetery wall,

the wild turkeys crossing the highway,
the leaves changing tones only
in the upper reaches of the branches,
and suddenly you are well again.

The sadness is red and yellow
and green and orange.
The sadness is a briefly passing wind
that holds the trees in its
Elysian embrace, allowing
them to let everything go

in a shower of beautiful release.

Atonement

Do you ever want to send out a blanket apology
to everyone you know?
I'm sorry. I know I disappeared or dropped the ball,
or I couldn't be exactly who you needed,
or I said something that hurt,
or I didn't show up,
or I took up too much space,
or I was a bit too confident
or angry or overwhelmed or done.
I am sorry for all those things.

Sending out a blanket letter of forgiveness, too.
I forgive you for disappearing or dropping the ball,
for not showing up,
for hurting me,
for misjudging me,
for taking too much space,
for being angry or overwhelmed or done.
I forgive you.

Can we begin again? I'd really like that.

Road Trip Medicine

Snacks and playlists,
audio books and small-town
sandwich shops, indie
bookstores, new rivers,
stunning views, and unexpected
connections with roadside
farmers.

Singing loudly,
layered conversations,
and so many stops
to take photos of the changing trees.

This is how you slow down time.
This is how you remember you're
alive and the world is still full
of such beautiful things.

Hurricane Season

Nature can be cruel,
raging out of control,
unconcerned with the damage it is doing.

Unstoppable forces remind us
that our greatest asset as human beings
is our ability to rely on one another.

It is our interconnectedness
that makes us so good at survival.

As many of our kin are watching
their homes and livelihoods washed away,
it is right to despair.
It is right to feel anger.

This is what empathy feels like.
Hold on to your ability to feel.
It's what grounds our humanity.

And we are so human.
Fragile alone. Unbreakable together.

Slow October Days

It is mid-October.
The night temps dip to near freezing,
and I turn the fireplace on in the morning
while I make my coffee in the dark.

The cat is hungry and then cold
and curls up full and happy on my lap.
She moves to the puzzle table
set up in front of the fireplace
and looks at me with a face that is ready
for the long, cold days ahead.

I dig out a warm winter hat
with a yellow poof on top
and plop it on Quillen's head
as he goes out the door to school.

The autumn light is dancing
through the half-empty tree branches
making jaunty patterns
on the green velvet of the sofa.

Years from now, I will look back
at these days, repetitive and calm,
with such soft eyes.
Poetry is one way to be nostalgic
about your life, even as it's happening.

Even as it's unfolding
uneventfully in front of you.
Even as these slow days
make up the very fabric of our lives together.

Fair Warning

Things are about to get
even more witchy,
more powerful,
less apologetic.

The Thinning Veil

When Alice goes through the looking glass,

when the key opens the secret garden,

when the One Ring is found,

when the tomb is found empty,

when the moon is full,

when the summer ends and darkness creeps in,

when magic and mystery dance with myth and poetry,

and we know, suddenly,

that there is more to the story, always.

When we lift the veil, the web is real.

Moving Through Liminal Space

As we come to the peak of fall,
I find myself between selves again.

This in-between place has become
as familiar to me as any fully embodied
version of myself ever is. Over the years,

I have built a little imaginary cabin
here in the liminal world,
with a wood-burning stove
and hardwood floors
and a forest of trees
that stretches to the horizon.

Here, I do not need to know who I am,
I can just exist in my multiplicities.

Migration

I can feel the lure of a new life
tugging at me like a chickadee
pulling fluff from the milkweed
that grows wild along the driveway.

I'm not sure where we would go,
but the cooler mornings
draw me magnetically toward the south—
buttered biscuits and peach jam,
unbothered conversations on the street corner,
and wide, covered porches with pitchers of iced tea.

I wish I were a Brewer's blackbird
or a giant Canadian goose,
migratory,
mobile,
allowed to follow the will of the wanderer.

I've never met a person more torn
between comfort and freedom
than I am,
caught between safety and longing,
between nesting and flight.

OCTOBER 31 (APRIL 30)

SAMHAIN/HALLOWEEN
Ritual of the Thinning Veil

This season is about endings, cycles, and death. Take some time to write about what's ending for you right now. Take a few moments to breathe into the pause of the season.

Do some meditation, either guided or moving or creative. Find a way to connect with those you have lost (in whatever way) and those in your life who have died. Write them a letter, or light a candle and just speak into it.

Rituals do not have to be complicated to be meaningful. Some other creative ideas for this week:

- Make a painting that speaks to the thin veil between this world, the fairy world, and the world of the dead.

- Write a poem to a loved one who died.

- Create a playlist that speaks to this season in your life.

- Get outside and do some nature studies in photography or drawing.

NOVEMBER

We need to spend less time in front of screens
and more time in front of campfires.

Of Darker Seasons

I am a woman of the darker seasons.
Let rainbow shades fade to brown and black.
Let crowded fields lie bare and open.

Let ancient winds rip through the soul
and whistling silence fill your lungs until
you know only truth in your bones.

Let honesty make its home
in your mind, clear as ice
and sharp as dragonfly wings.

Let breath fog up the window,
everything warm made visible,
every exhale a ghostly reminder
that you are alive.

Notes on Awe

I try to live as a child does,
in awe of every new thing.
Seeing the world as it is,
not as a memory of how it has been.

I take photographs on film
to capture the light on something real.
I visit every tree to document this time in their lives,
to notice how the trees respond to cold and wind,

to note how the leaves break down into mulch
within weeks, if left to do so.
I witness the bees dying on the flowers
and know that one day I will insist upon that kind of decay,

to be left where I have done the most good,
where my tending has been most consistent.

Slowing Down

She wraps herself in simple things—
in daily walks and easy conversations,
in loose clothes and sunlight,
in mindless TV and social media.

She wraps herself in ritual
to keep the world at bay,
measures out the sugar, the sweet cream, the tea,
the specific kind of heat that brings
her heart to a boil.

She wraps herself in moonlight and evening shade
and tends to those around her,
tries on new habits,
but one at a time,
one at a time.

My Body Knows What Heals It

a dark room and cool rain tapping on the roof.

an uninterrupted view to the horizon.

being fully heard.

curiosity,

love,

the simple act of creation,

be it drawing, photography, poetry

or life.

my body knows what heals it,

and mostly it's the simplest of things—

the sun,

my own sweet, unconditional love,

and time

to make something beautiful and true.

The Quiet Sounds of November

the window latching

the wood piling

the soup bubbling

the snow considering

the families gathering

the turkey basting

the dog sleeping

the Earth turning her face toward rest

Dear One,

I see you there with your fingers
clutching at life like a security blanket.
Soften, soften now to the possibility
that you must let something go.

Holding tightly will do nothing
but cut off the streams of love
that flow so tenderly, freely,
voluntarily around your rocky outcroppings.

You must surrender to the possibility of loss
so that the reality of love can exist without restraints.
Release your grip and your belief
that you can control the outcome.

Relax, unclench your fist, let go.
Breathe. Love. Repeat.

Embodiment Has Its Perks

Take the mountain pass

Roll the window down

Tell the stories that make you speed up with joy

Run your fingers through their hair

and tell them you can't stop thinking of their smile

Be so honest people call it refreshing

Ease into the river until it carries your grief downstream

Be gentle with your energy

Take a bath and stand looking at the full

harvest moon before the heat wears off

Let yourself fall in love again

Let yourself be enough for that

Oh, November

I lose my sense of self in November,
capture my face in photographs
as proof I still exist.

This month, with its waning light and
rising chill, takes my mind and spins it
like a doll with multiple expressions.

The other morning, I could hear myself think,
and it took all my effort to pull
myself out of the maelstrom of panic.

I choose, while I still can,
to drag my body toward the beam
of light coming in from Adams Street.

My dog barks at every car,
every child who rides by on a bike,
"There's someone there.
And there.
And there."

Rest and Be Weird

I'm no wiser, but I'm older,
and with that comes a certain
kind of certainty—

> that love is perennial,
>
> that rest will eventually add up to enough,
>
> that kindness is never wasted,
>
> and that being weird is just about

the best and most courageous way
to make friends for life.

When You Feel Alone

Make of yourself a warm place
for truth,
a place where honesty can rest
like a chicken from a fox.

Make of yourself a beacon
for everyone who is willing
to try,

for everyone willing
to face the discomfort of love
over and over again.

DECEMBER

Be joyful, create pathways,

live all the lives at once.

Be a light in the darkness.

Winter Has Plans of Its Own

As we enter into a time of winter,
we can feel the stillness beckoning.

Even as we celebrate, and decorate,
and sing.
Even as we wrap presents,
or light candles, or deck halls.
Even if we are mourning,
or lonely, or bereft,

the darkness is ours to rest in—
the winter has plans of its own.

Tucking In

As the darkest part of the year approaches,

I find myself sleeping more,

speaking less,

listening to the quiet

that settles over the yard.

I tuck into my couch,

light candles,

cuddle the cats,

reach for the stack of books,

and warm my feet by the fireplace.

As I age, there is more and more

comfort and ease in this time of the hermit.

Be Your Own Love

It's time to stop giving yourself away
and turn inward toward that burning hearth.
It's time to sit still and wait in warm waters
for your heartbeat to soften.
Lift your face to the sunbeam
and think about nothing
but the slowly shifting angle of the light.

Remember again that the truth can only exist
between you and your higher self,
she whom you met on a mountaintop in your mind.
It's time to pray only to her,
to the heart beating in your own chest.

Fingers interlaced in your own hair,
take all that big love
and place it gently on the sacred places inside,
until you remember who you are,
until the blueprint for your well-being
is etched like cave drawings
on the altar of your own soul.

I Love the Palette of December

Silver and red, green and gold.
Soft lighting, warm corners, and
greenery everywhere.

Popcorn in front of the fireplace
and warm socks, close animals.

The smell of cinnamon and cloves.

The winter world is a painting
of orange wincows in white houses
with black shutters—

and I, a poet, a housecat,
a dreamer, and a mother
am preparing
for the dark
with rhythm and twine.

On the Threshold of Winter

As we approach the longest night of the year,

amid the noise and the warm chaos of the season,

the hustle of planning,

the smells of cooking,

the joy and struggle of family,

the grief of those no longer with us,

I invite you to take this moment to listen.

Heed the inner voice within yourself

and let your soul catch up to your body.

In Love with Darkness

The first time I remember falling in love with darkness was during a meteor shower. It was my first year at camp in Northern Michigan and the sky was perfectly clear. We brought our blankets up to the top of a grassy hill and laid them out under the huge sky, full of stars.

We were up later than our scheduled bedtimes because the counselors didn't want us to miss the experience. And at first, we just watched the still sky and chatted and giggled as twelve-year-olds tend to do. I remember how hard the ground felt and how cold the air was. And then the meteors started streaking across the sky and the whole hill became silent as we lay transfixed by the sight.

It was a holy moment, a holy hour even.

DECEMBER 21–22 (JUNE 20–21)

YULE/WINTER SOLSTICE
Ritual of the Longest Night

Create a cozy gathering of friends and family. Have everyone bring a dark food, like decaf coffee and chocolate cake, rye bread, dark cherries, and aged cheese. Make a little picnic of your offerings.

Invite everyone to bring a book to read aloud. Have everyone curl up under a blanket. If you have a fireplace, create a hearth fire or a ring of candles. Tell stories, read poems, read a favorite chapter from a beloved children's story or fairy tale.

At midnight (or earlier if you'd like), turn off all the lights but keep one candle lit. A candle that is almost gone is best. Watch it until it flickers to nothing and allow yourselves to sit in darkness for a few moments.

Light a new candle to welcome in the winter.

You can offer this short meditation:

Imagine now that you are walking out of your home tonight. The laughter and the lights, the stress and the expectation of the holiday season fade into the distance as you wander into the darkness alone. You can perhaps see your breath, a white mist marking the inhale and exhale. The ground crunches lightly beneath your feet. A thin layer of frost sparkles in the moonlit expanse. You look up now and see a vast blanket of stars. They go on forever. And for a moment, you stand transfixed. You realize, perhaps, that you are standing on a huge floating ball, suspended in a sea of darkness. You can zoom out and see that you are on the dark side of the Earth, tethered to its surface by gravity alone. The mystery of life is connected so deeply to this slight tilt of the Earth. Our very existence now, as it always has been, is connected to how far away our little marble is from the sun. And so, as we begin our slow orbit back toward the sun, I invite you to pause in the darkness, unafraid, and create a holy moment for yourself, perhaps even a holy hour.

Winter Solstice

tangle up with darkness
and a love who sees you
clearly in any amount of light.

use only fire to guide you
through the silk of night.
let the edges be soft.
let the hallways gently flicker.

walk slowly toward the
river. let your body
move like water
rippling.

speak your deepest
truths to the moon
on her longest night.

breathe in the beauty
of winter.

let. everything. else. go.

It's Dusk Again

Time moves faster
than my soul
in winter.

I barely wake
and it is night
again.

Projects fall behind
and I sit with my
fresh brew

and ponder just
how gray the sky
can be.

Don't Forget to Listen

We are miraculous, mysterious
breathing, singing,
meaning-making
creatures of this Earth.

Don't forget to listen to each other.
Listen to your inner voice
and practice joy
and awe as often as you can.

Winter Lights

We become the map in winter,
our golden windows lighting up
our slow migration from the living room
to the bath, and then to the bed,
blinking on and off like fireflies.
"I love you," we say to each other.
"You feel so warm on my cold feet."

JANUARY

A new day is coming. This is always true.

JANUARY 1

NEW YEAR'S DAY
Ritual for Integration

Look back on last year and reflect on what worked and what didn't. When were you overwhelmed and wish you'd done less? When were you in a good flow with work and family and fun?

Go through your photos from the last year and create an album of your favorites (on your phone is fine). You can start to brainstorm some ideas for the coming year, but let yourself really take time to reflect and integrate before you charge ahead.

Happy New Year

Resolve only to

breathe more freely

more deeply

more soundly

into your own

sweet aliveness.

January Is For

fresh starts and promises
plans for the year
manifestations of our heart's desires
rest and recuperation from December
a time of fewer expectations.

Let winter settle in.
Tuck away the tinsel or the menorah,
the casserole dishes and the extra set
of sheets you keep for company.
Return again to yourself.
Nestle into darkness,
into early nights and hot cups of tea.
Journal by candlelight.
Get a cozy set of pajamas
and don't leave the house all weekend.

Plans for the Next Year

More rest

More laughter

More movement

More travel

More planting

More baking

More poetry

More gathering with purpose

More board games

More stretching

More vegetables

More walking

More listening

More acting with our values

More protecting our planet

More empathy

More compassion

More art

More love

Things I Want This Year

Easy conversation that flows

between depth and levity

Kindness in the eyes

and openness of the heart

Green spaces with lots of swings

and benches and shade

Art

Free public music

A focus on humanity over productivity

Appreciation of community

Time to gather and just be together

Familiar Beauty

Heavy snow in the branches
and a dazzling white that makes you
forget the gray of the day before.

The pink dawn rises like a sigh
over the clean lines
of the January roofs.

There is a flushed relief to familiar beauty,
a kind of solace that only habitual astonishment can bring.

Chiaroscuro

The snow lining the branches is white
charcoal on a gray background,
natural chiaroscuro.

I am taken into the arms of those black limbs
rising stark against the flat winter sky.

The window is a photograph
enlarged with dust left on the negative, and
everything is suddenly timeless.

Late January is such a slender feast,
a monochrome visage
of stillness.

Fear of Being Seen

When I'm all caught up
in the fear of being seen,
afraid of the judgment
and the loss that sometimes happens
when the world catches sight of my unruly self,

I turn my face to the sun.
I let the light from our closest star
warm my skin and imagine myself
as a tall and stalwart cedar.

I imagine the clouds come close
and shimmy into my branches,
The robin's nest in my sweet hollow places,
and nobody thinks to be cruel or afraid
of my true nature.

Like a rogue wave
rising suddenly out of calm seas,
I allow myself to be unexplainable.
Like a bittersweet seed,
I allow the possibility that I
am not to be consumed
by just anyone.

I Have a New Dream:

to wake up smiling,

to breathe in enough

of the pink-licked dawn

that I never need question

my worth by nightfall.

I'm feeling the need for simple pleasures today

Warm socks and hot coffee,
the stolen kiss of sunrise,
and the orange glow
of the neighbor's light
through the sycamore tree
that divides our properties.

I can hear the sound of the heat kicking on,
the pop of the pipes that signals more warmth.

I close my eyes and wrap the blanket tighter
around my shoulders.
I breathe deeply and remind myself
that I have time,

and not everything
needs to be figured out today.

The Woman Tending Fire

We're drawing down the clouds,
the sunlight and the moon,
the telephone wires, birdsong,
the harmonies, and drums.

We're calling in the wise ones,
the winged and the scaled,
the felines and amphibians,
the backboned and the tailed.

We're lifting up the timeline
to slide gently under the veil,
to the place where I have always lived,

in between the here and there.

We are the wandering liminal,
the poets and the guides,
the ancient woman tending fire
and the always-knowing child.

FEBRUARY

It is a strange thing
to allow a pause,
to trust that nothing is lost in my resting.

FEBRUARY 1–2 (AUGUST 1–2)

IMBOLC/DEEP WINTER

Where I live, February can be the harshest, coldest month of winter. That is why I love to celebrate the Celtic holiday of Imbolc, which marks the halfway point between the Winter Solstice and the Spring Equinox. This deep winter celebration reminds us that even though the ground is cold and frozen, the light is starting to return, life is still going deep within the earth, and soon spring will come again.

In the Celtic tradition, Imbolc is associated with Brigid, the goddess of fire, poetry, and the creative arts. Legend has it that Brigid's presence is especially potent during Imbolc, as she blesses the land with the first signs of spring and ignites the poetic flame within every soul.

Ritual of Poetry and Fire

Begin the ritual by taking a bath or washing your hands in warm water to symbolically clean and warm yourself. Then, light a candle or a small fire and gaze into the flame for a while.

Consider what you really want in life. Take a few moments to journal about the things you'd like to "light a fire under." What have you been putting off or feeling sluggish about? How can you more fully embrace your authentic, wild, poetic self?

When you're ready, take what you've written in your journal and turn it into a poem.

Soften Into Winter's Depths

The quiet flicker of the candle invites a sigh.

Perhaps beauty really is the antidote to despair,

to put pink roses in the window,

to pet the black curiosity in my lap,

to sip ginger tea

and watch the yard fill with

silent drifts of snow.

Begin Again and Again

When the world feels dire and dangerous,

we can see how community and art really are everything.

To have a place to gather,

to know a song to sing,

to read a poem that reminds you

that humans do this and survive.

Our "hobbies" become our salvation—

to bake bread and knit a sweater,

to grow herbs and tend wounds,

to have places to wait out the storm, the heat, the violence.

This is what humans do.

This is how we begin again and again, in love.

Wild Winter Woods

Follow the path of pine cones
through the pine red needles
until you find the clearing,

the place where fog reminds you
you were never alone.
Can you feel the rabbits breathing
deep beneath the earth?

The birds are pulling threads
from long-lost gloves
that hang from bare bush branches,

and you are here
in the wild winter woods,
nothing more than a creature
amongst creatures,

surrounded by Earth's beings,
safe
and sound
and free.

Tired One,

I wonder if you've breathed enough today.

If you've taken the time to press lightly on your closed eyelids, watching the fireworks ebb and flow across your inner landscape.

I wonder if you've turned off the screens and gone to the window, listening for the wind and the birdsong.

I wonder if you've eaten today. I often forget that part myself, until the headache comes and I unclench my jaw and lift the spoon to my lips.

I wonder if lying on the ground in your living room might feel nice. To lift your knees to your chest and rock back and forth.

I wonder if you can listen to music from your adolescence. Memory is so very powerful right now, so very comforting.

I wonder what makes you laugh, what tells your heart to grow instead of locking itself away. I wonder if you've cried enough . . .

Beloved creature, we have very few needs in the short term: air, water, food, shelter, and love. Tend to them first.

And then, don't forget to feel. Feel it all.

Valentine's Day

Be in love with your friends,
your pets, your children,
yourself.

Fall in love
with night drives
and glazed donuts
with your hot cup of coffee
your perfectly brewed tea
the freshly cleaned sheets
the bright bowl of lemons

the half-folded laundry
the sound of the neighbors
heading to work
with the way the light slants in
every morning and finds your
cat's closed eyes.

Fall in love with the world
and those you've chosen
to share it with,
imperfect but yours.

Hibernation Season

Be a cave dweller,

an earth burrower,

a fox warm in her den,

a rabbit waiting out the cold.

Be a fire-tender,

a soup-stirrer.

Live for the flicker of flames

and the smell of cedar burning.

Do not fear the stillness here,

the darkness, nor the cold.

There are songs only winter can sing,

and magic only February

can cast.

The Things That Warm You

When all is cold, turn toward the things that warm you—

the sun, a cup of Lady Grey, the dog with his small dog sighs,

the cat that settles in just as you need more coffee.

Memories, cookies, soup,

the future, in which we live more collectively.

Root vegetables,

tiny bookstores with a bell at the entrance.

Large coffee shops with couches and table lamps,

conversations about people you love,

the soft pants, the made bed,

the train ticket to Montreal.

The road trip, the old atlas

with every place you've been marked in red.

Bed Days

Some days
I work from bed.
I set everything up around me
a hot drink
a cold drink
tissues
notebooks
pens
my laptop
chargers.
I walk my dog
and feed the cats
and we all crawl in together,
various creatures at the headboard,
on my feet, at my side.

I have a body that needs
a lot of rest,
and learning how to love this
has been hard,
but my creatures teach me
how, soft bodies
breathing softly
together.

Torn

I've spent my life
torn between
insatiable wanderlust
and the desire to stay
under a blanket
with my tea
and a good book.

Self-Improvement

I say I want to read but I rarely read.
I say I want to move my body
but I sit for hours a day staring at my phone.
I say I want to work on my craft
but I can't bear to look at my work from the last year.

I want to cook but I order in again.
I want to dance but I watch crime dramas instead.
I want community but I hide and I hide and I hide.

How do we move from desire to action?
We get down deep, crouch into our bodies
and ask the question no one thought to ask,

"What do you really want, love?"
To be enough as I am.
To be enough as I am.
To be enough as I am.

MARCH

March is a half-frozen seed of hope.

A List of Things to Remember

Most of the time you can meet your own needs.

Walking in the woods solves more problems than you'd think.

Our hearts synchronize when we sing.

Your inner voice is not cruel; cruelty's voice is always someone else.

Animals know things.

We are animals.

We can sense the rain, a storm, the change of seasons.

We have a symbiotic relationship with plants; we need each other to survive.

Rest and time fix many, many things.

It is not too late for you to love your life.

Late Winter

I am drawn to the hidden things,
the squirrel tucked sleeping in the knot of a sycamore,
the underside of the frozen lake,
the unseen seeds awakening,
beneath the hard surface of the winter soil.

The spark of creativity that reignites
the coals of a memory you'd long forgotten,
the smell of your grandmother's quilt
as the snow piled like sugar against the house.

The old man in the far booth at Denny's at 1 a.m.,
counting out quarters for coffee,
laughing softly to himself.

The joys that come amidst the pain
of living with the knowledge
that we are but temporary beings
in a vast universe.

The Waking

I can feel my energy stirring,
twitching, turning,
little tendrils of aliveness
waking in the dark.

A slow, sly, smile
rising from the depths—
"I am here."

Waves

I go in and out, don't you?
Into flow and gratitude, and out of it again.
Into grief and hopelessness, and out of it again.
Into routine—cooking, walks, connection—

and then into bed, the bath, my head, my tears.
These days call for the ability to sway,
sway into reality, sway into empathy,
and back again.

Dip toes into fear, anxiety, awareness
and rest in creativity, distraction, comfort.

We go in and out, like tides
creating our own slow rhythms,
finding the pulse of survival.

In My Longing

I am the flow of an ice-cold river,
running fast over stones in the spring

I am a candle burning to its end.
I am a giant teal vase with lilacs bursting.
I am the perfect dining room table.

In my longing, I am useful,
not productive, not quantifiable,
but serving a purpose so clear
I don't doubt myself by nightfall.

In my longing, I am loved,
in my fatigue,
in my dread,
and in my genius.

I am held while I cry
about the insatiable hunger in the world,
the insatiable greed.

I am held in my complexity,
each tangled layer of thought,
feeling, intuition, knowledge.

Each world I create
will not be mine alone.

In my longing, I feel my multitudes as friends,

give each one a name,
a face,
an animal to guide them.

In my longing, it is a clear June day,
filled with the sweet scent of wet earth
and newly grown basil.
In my longing, we sit in comfortable silence,
whittling animals from wood,
nothing but the sound of the spring sparrows
and your happy sigh.

Imperfectly Divine

Place of deep longing in my heart,
find your way from silence to voice.
Give me strength and courage to speak truth through my life
for I am a creature of the Universe, small but infinite.
A momentary body in the sea of life, and also the sea itself.
I am a gathered bit of energy and one who gathers,
a creation and a creator.

Let me not hold too tightly to one form and lose the other.
We are not form but process, ever-changing and ever-renewing.
Help us see that we are neither the beginning nor the end,
but something perfectly natural and imperfectly divine.

Making Time

For those of us who
intentionally center mystery,
complexity, and paradox
at the heart of our lives,

we must make time
to grapple with unanswerable questions,
receive solace from the ever-present
hum of existence,

and just for a moment or two,
allow ourselves to be held
in that ineffable sense of love
and connection
of which we are all a part,

even if we cannot explain it.

MARCH 19–21 (SEPTEMBER 22–23)

OSTARA/SPRING EQUINOX

Ritual of New Beginnings

Developing a Spiritual Practice

What is a spiritual practice?

A spiritual practice is, at its core, a time in which you might have a spiritual experience (yes, even if you are someone who doesn't believe in anything supernatural). The intent is to help us reorient to the energy and life around us, to lift us out of the ordinary and automatic responses we have. Spiritual practices are a way of reminding ourselves of who we are and what our values are. They are about intention.

When thinking about developing a spiritual practice, remember that it needs to be something you can manage even at your lowest capacity, when the world has become quite bleak or overwhelming.

For me, that is a walk in the woods, or if I can't manage that (and sometimes I really can't), I take my shoes off and walk barefoot in my yard. It is a hot bath with a cup of tea. It is a guided meditation at bedtime. It is putting on a playlist full of songs from my adolescence and going for a drive at night. It is finding the moon between the houses. It is the extra five minutes I sit in the car before I come inside the house.

Take a few moments and think about some things you do or could do that bring you back to your best self, that give you time to experience awe or gratitude. And make a commitment to do more of those things.

Done with Winter

I crave a sunlit room
a picnic with fresh clementines
and sparkling cider
a clear night sky
and your lips on mine
your hand on my hips
the slow dance of
fireflies and cricket song.

I'm ready for the warm seasons,
outdoor concerts and soft
dresses. Ease, light, music.
Movement, new love, old
records, and the memory of
being young, played over
and over again.

An Incantation for Spring

Of foxes, ferns, and firmament
of earth and mud and candor

from roots to stem to dining room
we begin again and enter

a new season of vibrancy
of slush and sun and planting

come sow the seeds of poetry
and write the spring enchanted.

Nature Is Always a Way to Come Home

When you connect with the earth

through trees and wandering,

by planting seeds or

putting your feet in the ocean,

you connect with the infinite

parts of yourself,

the parts you cannot lose.

APRIL

Planting is my favorite way
to invest in the future,
my favorite way to feel small.

Thank You, Darkness

Thank your darkness now
for teaching you of rest
and grief and stillness.

Welcome back the light
who signs of joy and ease
and clarity.

The shift has come;
shake off the shadows
and emerge
whole and new.

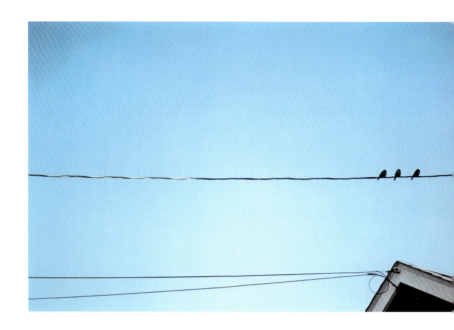

Welcome, Light!

Trust the energy that has felt

so elusive. It is real.

It is yours.

It is safe to play with,

to occupy,

to use as wings.

April Knows

April came with warm water
and the scent of cedar
with time spent writing
and oodles of fancy cheese.
It came with friends and games and a firepit.

It came with a knowing
that I can no longer pretend
to be someone I'm not
and hope to find what I'm looking for.

A letting go,
a bit of mourning,
a lot of joy,
and a prayer
that the world might take a turn toward hope.

Forgiveness

The light bouncing off the half-frozen lake
reminds me to be gentler with myself

to let the soft rays of the sun
become my salvation

to weaken the parts that have become hard
with grief and exhaustion.

Slowly relax my cells until they bend again
into water

until I forgive myself
for having been so cold.

Goals for April

Delve deeper

Breathe more freely

Embrace the lingering darkness

Collect kindred spirits

Empower ideas

Plant seeds of creativity

Hold space for transformation

Cultivate authentic communication

Channel creativity for spiritual growth

Spring Permission Slip

Suddenly I understood
that only I stand in my way,
that no one is holding a magic permission slip,
that permission is not granted for courage.

Courage exists in tiny moments
made explicit only through
the turn of the stomach.

The decision to sing loudly enough to be heard,
to write a poem and let someone read it,
to clear your calendar,
to turn down the job or accept it.

Rejection is a two-way door,
a kind of incision in the empty space
between the question and the answer.
I get to be the rejector
as well as the rejected,

and today, with the spring sun
falling in bright hallways through the window,
with my ear y '90s mix playing on Spotify,
I have finally figured out
how to choose a life for myself.

Details

Take one tiny thing
like the leaves you found
crushed in your jacket pocket from last season
or the ant crawling toward your child's cupped hands
a hair that crosses your lip repeatedly
while you're kissing your love
both of you smiling as you try to find it.

The smallest things tell the whole story.

A poem is just a moment made sacred with our noticing.

It's the End of April

and I am a woman inside her mind,
ignoring the needs of her body.

I am a woman in need of a fresh start,
a new pattern, a deeper breath and
quicker pace.

Can I change without destruction?
Can I ease into health without fixating on my body?
Can I find the balance between kindness and discipline?

When Your Mind Is Racing

Take a walk and look

for a single color to focus on—

yellow door

yellow leaves

the sun bouncing off the flooded street

a ticket left on the sidewalk from the school raffle

the bright voice of the sparrow

the daffodils and early daisies

bees

yellow miracles of attention

beckoning the ancient yellow buzz

of your animal heart.

Joy

Joy decided to join me today.

She had been hiding among the roots

in the vegetable garden.

She had been dancing

with frogs in the pond.

She had been ice skating

around the frozen tundra

on the other side of the world.

And I had almost forgotten her warm harmonies.

The way she makes everything lighter.

I could hear her whistling through

the deepening green of spring branches,

and I felt soft breezes

caress my tender heart.

My brow softened

and my jaw unclenched

and I welcomed her home

with a sigh.

MAY

My heart is doing that thing
where it blooms
all of a sudden.

MAY 1 (NOVEMBER 1)

BELTANE/MAY DAY
Ritual of Flowers

Halfway between the Spring Equinox and the Summer Solstice sits May Day (or Beltane or Floralia), a celebration of the beginning of the warmer seasons, when the cattle could be brought out to pasture and the world began to burst into bloom.

I invite you to fill your home with fresh flowers, make floral drinks, and drink in the relief of late spring.

Free to Choose

Return to the self, beloved.
Return to the well and drink deeply
of the sacred knowledge of your wholeness.

Light the fire of your enoughness
and warm your toes by its crackling twigs.
When you've lost your way,
just sit still for a moment.

This life has given you many wounds,
both your own
and those of your ancestors.
There may be a frantic, terrified lineage inside you
that has no idea what safety feels like.

But you are safe,
and you can remember it for them.
You are free.
You are safe.
You are free to choose.

What Has Been Eclipsed Is Shifting at Last

The earth sings a song of blossoms
and generosity, and I reach
for one more handful
of bread, one more ripe
orange, one more kiss.

My hand on your chest
pulling you closer
than the full moon
standing watch
outside our window.

I become the insatiable
birdsong, the outrageous
white blossoms against
that blue sky. I open
again and the world rushes
in like seawater through
the beating heart.

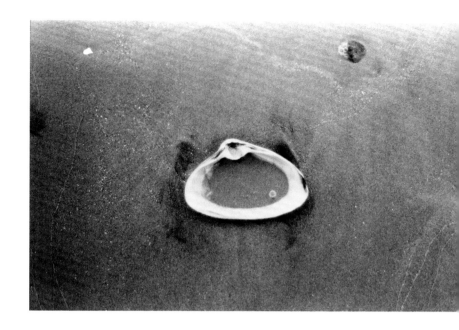

Wholeness Party

When you feel depleted, close your eyes
and reach for the tender parts of yourself
that linger with those you've loved,
and gently (sc gently) invite them home.

Their return will feel like sunshine.
Embrace each piece
and give them honey cakes and lemonade.
Throw a party for your wholeness.

It Must Be Spring

I am a sudden rush
of crushes. It must
be Spring. Luscious
tendrils of desire
push through the hard
winter places.
I think of your hands
and open.
I remember your hands
and blush.

At the Edge of the Lake

I gasp at the simplicity

of this kind of beauty—

water,

tree line,

fog.

A miraculous portal of peace

opens within

and reminds me

just how easy it can be

to feel free.

Thorns

Every time I find myself on the mat
beating myself senseless with
my own judgment
I take my body to the woods.

I walk among the gnats and mosquitoes
I bask in the dark green sunlight
and walk until the voices become
my footsteps

quiet and rhythmic.

I walk until I love myself again
until the earth reminds me that
every living thing has a stinger
or a barb

that survival isn't always sweet
and self-protection is an
inevitable consequence of
sharing breath with a sometimes
hostile world.

I walk until I become the rose or
the milk thistle
thorny yet beautiful
allowed to hurt sometimes.
allowed to demand more space to grow.

A New Season

I've spent years chasing intensity
and recovering from it.
To feel the elation of infatuation,
the allure of something new to learn,
the multitudes of places to see.

Now I am in a season
of moderation and mundanity.
And this, too, has an intensity to it.

I watch the sweet peas slowly curl
around the metal climbing structure
and pluck the kale from the earth as it's ready.
I slice the lemons into a glass,
add sparkling water and sugar.

I brush my son's wild hair
and make the same lunch every day.
I kiss the same mouth each night and call it good.

This, too, is something new for me,
something worthy of obsession.

Mother's Day

For everyone who mothers
on this complicated day,
may you know your worth
does not depend on perfection.
May you believe you are allowed to rest,
may your needs be met consistently,
may you feel loved and nurtured
as you love and nurture those
around you.

For the Many Ways We Mother

Mother is warm breezes
and firelight,
tender hands
that fasten laces
buttons and buckles.

She tucks loose dreams
into her pockets to
reminds us who we are
when we've forgotten.

She is the weaver of
safety and courage,
of fierce love
and open arms.

She is the voice inside us,
the lantern that guides us,
the moon with her steady gravity
safely holding the seas.

Mother is creation herself,
the choice to nourish
what needs our love most dearly,
the tender, growing things
of this world.

Adventure Is Small Things

All I want is midnight kisses
with the man who puts our
child back to bed for the third time
in one night.

Adventure is in these small things—
being willing to stay tuned in,
to listen to the all of someone.

To see past the hopes and fantasies
to the heart and soul of a human being,

scared and sacred at once.

JUNE

I want the light of summer
to make our darkest places
feel safe to explore.

Summer Is Here

Allow yourself to shed the masks you've worn
since you knew how to speak.
You found ways to protect yourself,
to keep your young self safe,
to make a space for them far from harm.

You are not a child now,
and you know how to choose.

Open yourself to the right kind of people.
You can sense smiles that hide dangerous teeth.
You have teeth of your own.

Put down your daggers and tend to the campfire,

the heat, the heart, the children.

You can sing freely now,
like the birds, for survival is done
and summer is here.

Long-Term Love (Marriage Season)

We poets like to write
about the first rush of love—
the dilated pupils,
or the quickly beating heart,

the awakening of pieces
of ourselves never before discovered,
the way every song on the radio is
suddenly just for you.

New love is a glorious thunderclap,
a crackling revelation in the dark.

By the time we come to marriage,
we have a different understanding.

We begin to see
how everything real
takes its time—

love most of all.

Long-term love
is a dance
between safety and freedom.
It's the joy of knowing another deeply,
but never losing curiosity for who
they are becoming.

It's asking for help.
It's learning to argue.
It's car maintenance
and school runs.

It's doing the taxes
and making the coffee
(even when it's not your turn).
It's listening to the same story
again, with only slight variations.

Long-term love
is showing up
again and again,
to the table, the conversation,
the dance floor,
the shared life,
and saying every year—
I still choose this.
I still choose us.

The Rhythm of Summer

When it's hot,
wake early.
Walk before the sun rises
over the willow tree.

Listen to the doves and chickadees,
a symphony of gladness and trust.
Take it slowly, drink more water.

As the day takes over, eat bowls
of fresh cherries and plums,
pluck sweet peas from the vine.

Find the shade, the river,
the glade, the thrum,
and ease into the rhythm

of summer.

Small Comforts

(after Katha Pollitt)

The metal tables in coffee shops, the soft chatter of company,

the way the sun shines in your hair in golden halos,

illuminating the edges of your facial features.

The crickets beginning to chirp in the early dusk evenings of summer.

A picnic blanket thick enough to shield your ankles from hard tree roots.

The crisp snap of an aluminum can opening.

Bare feet on the back deck,

the slamming of the screen door, and

the sound of children laughing.

The tuning of guitar strings and friends

trying to find the right note to begin the song.

The alchemy of music and memory,

how a single chord can evoke an entire season of love,

or loss, or a whole city, a beloved person,

a version of ourselves we almost forgot.

Our minds are full of small comforts

we can trap deep in our bones,

to light the way later in the year.

Devotion

I devote myself to peace,
to contemplation,
to the trees.

I devote my life to creativity,
to creating places of belonging,
to justice.

I devote my time to peaceful things—
writing, love, learning,
growing, mothering,
tending home,
art, friendship,
community.

Father's Day

For everyone who fathers,
may you know your
warmth and vitality are as important
as your stability and success.

May you know your sweet
heart, with its grief and tenderness,
is part of what makes you
strong enough to parent.

May you feel how loved
and treasured you are
today and every day,
not just for what you do,
but for who you are.

What Lights You up on Late June Days?

My life, my dreams,

the way light hits the kitchen table,

my loves, my friends,

the foxgloves

and the pine trees,

the geese and how ridiculously amazing

cherries are,

travel,

the moon,

a road that bends,

old photographs,

attraction,

the way time just can't be real.

Everything. Everything. Everything.

JUNE 20–22 (DECEMBER 21–22)

LITHA/SUMMER SOLSTICE

Ritual of the Longest Day

Moonlight Dance Party

At sunset, toast the longest day with something delicious (I like sparkling apple juice in a beautiful goblet). Invite the moon to dance with you. Play a song or two that brings you joy and do a little frolicking. This can be done alone or with a small group of people you feel safe being silly with. The important thing is to embrace the part of you that is wild and free and allow yourself to be completely present to this first summer night.

The Midsummer Fairy

The Midsummer Fairy wakes after dark
on the longest day of the year
to share her wisdom and mischief with me.

She places plums in my pockets
and teaches me new ways
of playing human for another year.

We share our truths
and call them fiction.
We sing the same song
in our heads.

We dance wildly together
under a strawberry moon
while the trees pretend to sleep.

Meet Me in 1997

Let's drive to Blockbuster
with the windows down
blasting Ani DiFranco's "Untouchable Face."
Take an hour to pick out movies,
one old and one new.
Buy Raisinets and microwave popcorn
at the cash register and have a truly
unremarkable evening in your parents'
basement. We can drive home
the long way and stop in the park
to make out and split our last
Camel Light, side by side on the swings,
the only sound that metallic creaking
back and forth.

Summer Dreams

Of fireflies and fireworks,
swimming pools and
cold creek water,
smooth stones and minnows
that touch bare feet with curiosity.

Road trips and mix tapes,
car games and rest stops,
until at last,
the smell of the sea,
after miles and miles of mountains.

JULY

Every summer, I find myself again.

So, Apparently I'm a Soft Summer

the perfectly ripe nectarine

the slightly firm avocado

the trees shaking water off in the wind

like a wet dog after a rainstorm

the sound of flies bumping into glass

the weeds so tall and thick they've

staked their claim

as a stubborn toddler might do

refusing to go to up the stairs for bed

Summer's Soundtrack

The yard is a feast of green
and the zucchini is in blossom.
Wildflowers grow taller than the clover
and bunnies leap with mouths full
when I open the back door.

I prayed myself here,
I dreamed and worked and got lucky
in this lifetime,

to live where I can hear the wind
in the trees, the bright scratch
of the crows calling to each other,
the hollow woodwind of the single
dove cocing his good morning song.

The soundtrack of summer is
so familiar in my chest,
like the rush of blood
after a hot bath, or the
predictable tone of my son's
voice, calling out for me.

In(ter)dependence Day

It is summer and I want to celebrate
that my neighbor speaks English and Spanish
in the same sentence,
that I can read any book I want,
that my body is mine
to fling into the lake or walk freely
down the street without fear.

I want to celebrate with potlucks,
block parties, fusion dancing,
and poetry. With laughter
and community, cookouts
and accountability.

While we celebrate the hard-won
freedom we gained,
please also remember
that it is our interdependence
not just our independence
that makes this life worth
fighting for.

Peach Season

I'm such a screened-in porch on a hot summer day kind of girl,
a cold water, sparkles on the lake kind of girl,
a table full of taco toppings and fresh tortillas kind of girl,
a wake up early and drink your coffee
around the remnant of last night's fire kind of girl.

I am a woman of sunlight and wildflowers,
of peaches and daisy chains,
of June, July, and August.

July Is Too Hot to Work

July isn't for production.
It's for fresh plums and bare feet.
It's for rope swings over glistening lakes,
for laughter and freshly laundered towels.
July is for lemonade and late-night strolls,
large-brimmed hats,
and the scent of sunscreen and roses.
July would like you to take five things off your to-do list,
make a space in your calendar
so large you could drive through it,
windows down, playlist on, and a lazy dog
panting in the passenger seat.

Summertime Slow

Summer is for staying up late

and eating outside,

kissing slowly while

the sun hangs on,

setting as lazily as

your hands

gliding down my back.

Flavor of Joy

Let yourself ripen on the vine.

Sunlight, water, stillness, safety.

Growth comes when we are fed.

Change comes when we stop trying so hard to become.

Turn your face to the sun and drink it in.

Soak up the rain.

Don't hurry maturation—

you are the perfect flavor of joy

right this moment.

Sunlight's Message

Move toward fresh fruit
Bare feet
Laughter.

I Dream of a House in the Woods

Silvermist mornings and rocking-chair coffee.
The sound of rain on the screened-in porch.
A quiet, unencumbered view . . .
horses, warm and dry, in the barn down the hill,
and maybe some chickens, pecking
the ground at our feet.

A New Archetype

Become the eccentric older woman
you've always been on the inside.

Wear outrageous clothes and live in a house
with jewel-toned rooms and magazines piled high,
art hung on the walls made by painters you knew
in your Parisian phase.

Show the world your collection of animal bones
and tarot cards, get a couple more cats,
raise a wolf pup from birth,
swim naked in the dark and glistening water.

Turn the page and leave everything known behind,

create a new archetype—the one they'll tell their
children about, the one who didn't have to compromise,
the one who lived free
and stayed alive
and loved.

AUGUST

What if the best is far from over,
and even now, the scales are tipping
toward more joy?

AUGUST 1 (FEBRUARY 1)

LAMMAS/HARVEST SEASON

Ritual of Bounty

Late Summer Feast

Invite friends and/or family over and have dinner outside. Make beautiful food, using vegetables and fruits that are in season. Play with color and texture. Take photos of the feast!

Light some candles as it gets dark and take turns saying one thing you're grateful for.

Summer Feet

Summer feet know every surface
the shores of the river bed
and the sand of the ocean shore
the grass and clover of the backyard
the hardwood floor of the kitchen
the dog's fur, the lover's sheets
the hammock gently swinging on the back porch
the wind, the sun, the earth, the water
summer is the closest we get to becoming
the animals we once were, nearly naked and
living off the land with handfuls of blueberries
and our feet connecting us to the earth

Season of Joy

Sand on skin,

the smell of sunscreen,

bare feet running

down wooden planks to the sea,

laughter echoing off white waves

as the sun rises over a blue horizon.

You remind me of summer mornings,

bigger than a single moment.

You are an entire season of joy.

Vacation Season

August is for camping

trail mix and sunscreen

the slow hike through the deep green

the unparalleled view to the horizon

sweatshirts that smell of dirt

and campfire smoke

the memory of songs drifting up

into the arms of Orion

and the sound of laughter

echoing in the canyon.

To be home again

and make the coffee
the way I like it, black
as I like my bedroom
at night.

To sit in my chair
and wait for my cat
to settle,

as she does every morning,
the light streaming in
from the huge front window.

We are both still,
and quiet,
and happy.

Frivolous

Salt water, sweat, and a surrender to what is.
August is a time for basking in the beauty of too much heat.

Simple, simmering, sunlight and wet children laughing.
Picnics and fireflies.

August asks our lives, What if it was easy?
What if it was playful, joyful,
and unencumbered by the illusion of "goodness"?

What if our living could be as blithe as a beach read?

Summer asks,
What if the best of what we have to offer lives inside the permission of frivolity?

Don't Skip Ahead

I know the cool air
and crisp apples of
fall are beckoning sweetly
while the mosquitoes hum
around the ripe tomato plants.

I know the kids are restless
and done with camp and the
days loom longer and bright
and ungodly hot at times.

But August is the moment.

It is the juiciest peach,

the laughter coming off the lake,
the last few pages of your summer read,
the sound of ice clinking in a glass.

It is the perfect time to teach yourself
how to be bored again.
What did you love to do as a kid?
When the TV was off and the phones
weren't as smart?

Did you ever just sit on the stairs
in front of your house and listen
to the neighbor kids playing basketball?

Just that,
bounce,
bounce,
and the moon
slowly rising above the horizon?

Move like Water

When August's lack of routine
starts to wear on your nerves,
when the sun is too bright,
the days still too long,
and the wet, heavy heat
makes you feel wilted and slow,

it is time to move like water,
languidly, lazily through the landscape.
Give up all sense of urgency or time
and float, arms open,
under the dark green leaves
of the summer trees.

It's August in New England.

The day is heavy with heat,
the tomatoes are ripe on the vine,
and nothing is hurrying.

We are all languidly lounging,
until the cool of night sets in
with her brilliant breezes
and lightly rapping raindrops.

Be the cat stretching out wide on the hardwood floor.
Be the dog watching the children ride bikes down the street.
Be the bees restlessly humming in the black-eyed Susans,
the wind running its wild hands
through the green branches of the willow tree.

The End of Summer

I am trying to remember how to be joyful,
not just accomplished.
How to be inspired again by the silver moon
and the clouds surrounding her in a ring.

The room is filled with my fear of aging,
with pets that need a quick trip to the vet,
with dental appointments and eye exams.
My life becomes a list of things I need to schedule
and cancel and reschedule and dread,
and I just want to drive until I find a field of sunflowers.

Pick peaches before it's too late.
Make apple butter and pumpkin pie.
I want to stop racing around in a panic
about the things I should be doing
and read on the front porch
while the last of the summer days are here,

Come away from the window of anxiety
and imposter syndrome
and rest with me a moment.

Pull your mind back from the teethy places and look around you.
The sky is full of Georgia O'Keefe clouds,
your plants are still alive and growing,
the air is cool and the room is warm,
and nothing is actually wrong.

Small and Wondrous

When the world is overwhelming,
too loud, too bright, too much,
turn toward the quiet within
your own, sweet body,
to the steady pull of Earth's gravity,
the rhythmic beat of your miracle heart.

Breathe in the crisp morning air
and listen for the sounds of your life—
the coffee maker percolating,
the train whistle somewhere in the distance,
the morning dove cooing,
the sound of footsteps on the stairs.

Tune in to the small and wondrous sounds of your life
and name them within intention.

I choose this.
I choose right now.
I choose today.

ABOUT THE AUTHOR

Alix Klingenberg is a poet, artist, and earth-centered spiritual director living with her family (and a house full of pets) in Melrose, Massachusetts. With a bachelor's degree in visual art from Oberlin College and a master's in divinity from Meadville Lombard Theological School, Alix weaves professional photography, mysticism, personal narrative, and a bit of ecological justice into her work. You can find her creative classes and essays on Substack, at Earth & Verse, and more of her visual poetry on Instagram @AlixKlingenberg.

An Imprint of MandalaEarth
PO Box 3088
San Rafael, CA 94912
www.MandalaEarth.com

Publisher Raoul Goff
Associate Publisher Roger Shaw
Senior Editor Peter Adrian Behravesh
Assistant Editor Amanda Nelson
Creative Director Ashley Quackenbush
Senior Designer Stephanie Odeh
VP Manufacturing Alix Nicholaeff
Senior Production Manager Joshua Smith
Strategic Production Planner Lina s Palma-Temena

MandalaEarth would also like to thank Crystal Erickson.

Text and photographs © 2025 Alix Klingenberg

All rights reserved. No part of this book may be reproduced in any form without written permission from the publisher.

ISBN: 979-8-88762-153-1

Manufactured in China by Insight Editions
10 9 8 7 6 5 4 3 2 1

Insight Editions, in association with Roots of Peace, will plant two trees for each tree used in the manufacturing of this book. Roots of Peace is an internationally renowned humanitarian organization dedicated to eradicating land mines worldwide and converting war-torn lands into productive farms and wildlife habitats. Roots of Peace will plant two million fruit and nut trees in Afghanistan and provide farmers there with the skills and support necessary for sustainable land use.